PICTURE A COUNTRY

Czech Republic

Henry Pluckrose

W
FRANKLIN WATTS
A Division of Grolier Publishing
NEW YORK • LONDON • HONG KONG • SYDNEY
DANBURY, CONNECTICUT

This is the Czech flag.

Photographic acknowledgements:

Cover: Top right, Robert Harding (Michael Short), bottom right (above) and bottom left, Robert Harding (Gavin Hellier).
Insides: AA p.22; Arcaid p.14 (Richard Bryant); Axiom Photographic Agency pp. 11b, 20, 21t, 21b (D. Shaw); Bridgeman Art Library p.26 (Národní Gallery, Prague); Bruce Coleman p.12 (Atlantide); James Davis Travel Photography p.28r; Getty Images p.28l (Stephen Studd); Robert Harding Picture Library pp. 9, 10, 13 (James Strachan), 11t, 15 (Gavin Hellier), 19t (Liba Taylor), 25b (Michael Short), 27 (Robin Hanbury-Tenison); Hutchison Picture Library p. 25t (Liba Taylor); Images p.29 (Horizon/Adina Amsel Tovy; Impact p.23 (John Cole); Panos p.16 (Liba Taylor), 17t (Trygve Bolstad); Popperfoto p.24 (Dave Joiner); Skishoot-Offshoot p.8 (J. Lucas); Skoda/VW Group UK Ltd p. 17b (); Still Pictures p. 18 (Andre Malennikov).
All other photography by Steve Shott.

Map by Julian Baker.
Series editor: Rachel Cooke
Editor: Alex Young
Series designer: Kirstie Billingham
Picture research: Sue Mennell

First published in 1999 by Franklin Watts
First American edition 1999 by
Franklin Watts
A division of Grolier Publishing
90 Sherman Turnpike
Danbury, CT 06816

Visit Franklin Watts on the Internet at:
http://publishing.grolier.com

Pluckrose, Henry Arthur.
    Czech Republic / Henry Pluckrose.
        p. cm. -- (Picture a country)
    Includes index.
    Summary: A simple introduction to the geography, people, culture, and interesting sites of the Czech Republic.
    ISBN 0-531-14512-3
    1. Czech Republic--Pictorial works--Juveline Literature.
[1. Czech Republic.] I. Title. II. Series: Pluckrose, Henry Arthur. Picture a country.
DB2013.P58 1999
943.71--dc21   98-30779
                                                      CIP
                                                       AC

GROLIER
PUBLISHING

Contents

Where Is the Czech Republic?

This is a map of the Czech Republic. The Czech Republic is a small country in Central Europe, bordered by Germany, Poland, Austria, and Slovakia.

Here are some Czech stamps and money.

Czech money is counted in Krone.

The Czech Landscape

The Czech Republic is made up of two main areas — Bohemia in the west and Moravia in the east.

Winter snow covers Korenov in the Krkonose (or "Giant") Mountain range in northern Moravia.

A barge floats down the River Elbe near Ustí nad Labem in northern Bohemia.

There are four large rivers that run through the hilly Czech countryside: the Moldau, the Beraun, the Eger, and the Elbe. These rivers are important because the Czech Republic has no borders with the ocean.

In the summer the weather is wet and warm. In the winter the weather can be very cold.

The Czech People

A people called the Slavs have lived in Eastern Europe for hundreds of years. There are many kinds of Slavs. Most people in the Czech Republic are Czech Slavs. There are also Slovak, Polish, Russian, and Ukrainian Slavs living in the Czech Republic.

This boy is wearing a traditional Czech costume.

Today over 10 million people live in the Czech Republic. Three different languages are spoken — Czech, Moravian, and Slovak.

Most Czechs live in small towns in the countryside, like the town of Vranov nad Dyjí in southern Moravia.

Where They Live

Ceské Budejovice is a large town in southern Bohemia. About 97,000 people live there.

Most Czech people live in small towns and villages. There are some large towns — Brno, Ceské Budejovice, Ostrava, and Teplice.

The Capital City

Prague is the capital of the Czech Republic. Over 1 million people live there.

This building looks like a dancing couple. It is named "Fred and Ginger" after two famous dancers.

The Moldau River runs through the center of Prague. The two sides of the city are joined by many bridges.

Prague is an ancient city with many beautiful buildings, museums, and parks.

At Work

This man is making a crystal (glass) vase at a factory in north Bohemia.

Many Czech people work in factories. They make steel, pottery, glass, and cars. Mining is also important. The Czechs mine for coal, iron, silver, and graphite.

Nearly 5,000 people work in this steel factory in Kladno.

Skoda cars are made in the Czech Republic.
They are sold all over the world.

Farming

Czech farmers grow cereal crops such as barley, oats, rye, and wheat. They also grow green vegetables, sugar beets, fruit, and potatoes.

This man is putting hops into a copper brewing kettle to make beer.

The Czech Republic is famous for its beer. A crop called hops is grown to make beer. The hops give the beer its strong flavor.

19

Home and School

At home, Czech families spend their time much like you. Meal times are important for families, and friends are always welcome. Czech children start nursery school when they are very young. They do not start elementary school until they are seven.

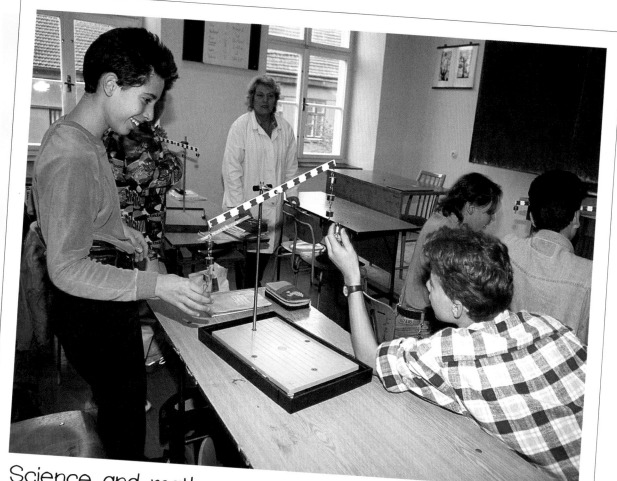

Science and mathematics are an important part of schoolwork in the Czech Republic.

This boy is in a woodworking class.

Czech Food

Czech people enjoy all kinds of food: chicken, bacon, ham, pork, eggs, fresh fruit, and vegetables.

A favorite meal is *vepro-knedio-zelo* — roast pork, cabbage, and small balls of dough called dumplings.

Duck, red cabbage, and potato pancakes make a traditional Bohemian meal.

Fruit and vegetables grown in the countryside are sold in town and city markets, like this one in Prague.

Doughnuts are also popular.
They are often filled with apples,
plums, or cheese.

Out and About

Czech people play many kinds of sports: golf, tennis, soccer, and ice hockey.

People also like to go to concerts, and puppet shows are always popular.

The Czech ice hockey team is often very successful in the World Championships.

Outdoor concerts take place in the summer. They may include music by the Czech composers Dvorák or Janácek.

Churches and Festivals

The Czech Republic has many old churches filled with beautiful things.

This tapestry was made for a church in the 14th century.

These girls are dancing around a maypole to celebrate the beginning of summer.

There are festivals throughout the year, such as Christmas, Easter, and May Day. People celebrate by dancing, feasting, and giving gifts.

Visiting the Czech Republic

Each year thousands of tourists visit the Czech Republic.

This clock in Prague started telling the time in 1410.

This beautiful building houses the warm water springs in the spa town of Mariánské Lázne in Western Bohemia.

People come to see Prague, as well as other beautiful places, such as the spa towns. A spa is a town built around warm water springs. People think swimming in or drinking the water can cure diseases.

Index

About This Book

The last decade of the 20th century has been marked by an explosion in communications technology. The effect of this revolution upon the young child should not be underestimated. The television set brings a cascade of ever-changing images from around the world into the home, but the information presented is only on the screen for a few moments before the program moves on to consider some other issue.

Instant pictures, instant information do not easily satisfy young children's emotional and intellectual needs. Young children take time to assimilate knowledge, to relate what they already know to ideas and information that are new.

The books in this series seek to provide snapshots of everyday life in countries in different parts of the world. The images have been selected to encourage the young reader to look, to question, to talk. Unlike the TV picture, each page can be studied for as long as is necessary and subsequently returned to as a point of reference. For example, Czech industry might be compared with that in their own local area, or a discussion might develop about the ways in which food is prepared and eaten in a country whose culture and customs are different from their own.

The comparison of similarity and difference is the recurring theme in each of the titles in this series. People in different lands are superficially different. Where they live (the climate and terrain) obviously shapes the sort of houses that are built, but people across the world need shelter; coins may look different, but in each country people use money.

At a time when the world seems to be shrinking, it is important for children to be given the opportunity to focus upon those things that are common to all the peoples of the world. By exploring the themes touched upon in the book, children will begin to appreciate that there are strands in the everyday life of human beings that are universal.